Windows On Beginning Science
Active Learning for Young Children

Water and Ice

Joan Westley

Creative Publications

Project Manager: Micaelia Randolph

Edited by Ann Roper

Illustrated by Jane McCreary

Cover design by JoAnne Hammer

Cover illustration by Jane McCreary

©1988 Creative Publications
788 Palomar Avenue
Sunnyvale, California 94086
Printed in U. S. A.

ISBN: 0-88488-708-1

7 8 9 10. 9 5 4 3 2

Table of Contents

Notes to the Teacher

What is *Windows on Beginning Science?*

Windows on Beginning Science is a hands-on science program created especially for young children, prekindergarten to grade two. The content focuses on everyday things such as water, light, bugs, seeds, sand and rocks, and ramps and wheels. By participating in a series of motivating and problem-solving investigations, children are guided to explore, observe, discover relationships, record, and communicate their observations about the world about them.

The activities in *Windows on Beginning Science*:

- provide a complete range of science skills and processes across familiar topics in life, earth, and physical science;

- can enrich any other science materials you may currently have in place;

- can be used to build integrated units involving science, language arts, mathematics;

- correlate very well with Windows on *Mathematics*™.

The *Windows on Beginning Science* program consists of six resource books that cover topics in life, earth, and physical science:

> Seeds and Weeds
> Insects and Other Crawlers
> Rocks, Sand, and Soil
> Water and Ice
> Constructions
> Light, Color, and Shadows

A separate Management Guide includes a skills inventory, materials list, safety tips, reproducible masters for Sorting Mat activities and Data Sheets. A *Windows on Beginning Science* Complete Materials Kit is also available. See Catalog. No. 56933.

What is the philosophy of the program?

Windows on Beginning Science emphasizes the development of scientific thinking rather than the acquisition of specific scientific principles. The program is based on the premise that young children will learn best about the nature and processes of science when they:

- Actively explore materials first-hand in open-ended investigations,

- are guided by thought-provoking questions,

- are encouraged to describe their observations and discoveries to others,

- are given many opportunities to record their observations in a variety of meaningful ways, (experience stories, drawings, graphs, tables, poems, and so on).

How is the program organized?

Each *Windows on Beginning Science* resource book is divided into 28 investigations. Each investigation is called a "window." A window is designed to be used with a small group of children and should take approximately one science period to complete unless otherwise specified. The windows are sequenced by difficulty—the simpler activities occurring first in any one book. It is not essential, however, to use the activities in order from beginning to end. The Table of Contents lists all windows and their objectives so you can skim through first and then choose the lessons you wish to use.

Each activity consists of two facing pages. The left-hand page lists the title of the activity, a summary statement describing the investigation, the skills, the necessary materials, and how to set up for instruction. There is also an illustration that shows the activity in action.

The right-hand page is divided into three sections: Starting Out, Guiding Children's Actions, and Stretching Their Thinking.

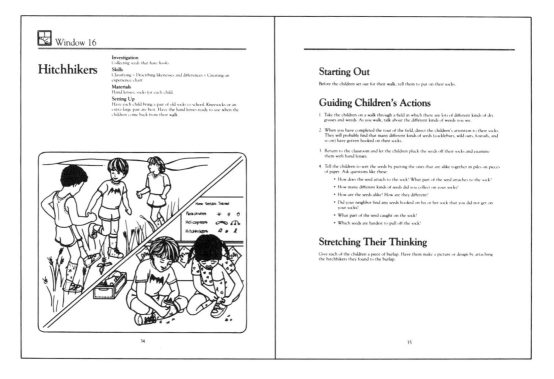

Starting Out presents a warm-up activity, challenge, or question to capture the children's interest and get them underway on the activity.

Guiding Children's Actions is the core of the activity. It provides step-by step instructions for conducting the activity. All instructions are clearly numbered and specific questions are provided for directing children's thinking.

Streching Their Thinking provides a variation of the basic activity and is designed to extend students' thinking. It may follow the basic activity on the same day or it may be presented on another day.

What about safety?

Safety is an important aspect of any science program. The activities in *Windows on Beginning Science* have been carefully developed with safety in mind and when used with appropriate supervision and reasonable care, pose no safety hazards for children. However, before starting any activity, it is always good to review the do's and don'ts of handling the materials involved. When necessary, specific safety tips are included in the *Windows on Beginning Science* resource books. We also recommend you refer periodically to the general safety guidelines in our *Windows on Beginning Science* Management Guide. (Cat. No. 56930)

An excellent reference on science safety entitled *Safety in the Elementary Science Classroom* can be ordered from the National Science Teachers Association. The address is:

> National Science Teacher Association
> 1742 Connecticut Avenue N.W.
> Washington, D.C. 20009

About Water and Ice

Children experiment with bubbles, paper boats, and rainbows. They try to mix oil with water, and discover the joys of marbled paintings and crayon resist. In addition, they explore dissolving, absorbing, melting, and freezing.

Water Is Different

Investigation
Comparing water to sand and rice.

Skills
Describing likenesses and differences ◊ Using the sense of touch ◊ Creating experience charts ◊ Comparing weight

Materials
Plastic wash tubs; sand; water; rice; plastic funnels; measuring cups; measuring spoons; plastic bottles; paper towels; large paper for experience chart.

Setting Up
Set up a pouring center. The center should have three tubs, one containing water, one containing rice, and one containing sand. Separate the tubs so the children will not inadvertently combine the materials. Provide plastic funnels, measuring cups, measuring spoons, bottles, sieves, and so on. Prepare an experience chart with the headings *Rice*, *Sand*, *Water* as shown and set aside.

Starting Out

Let the children freely explore the properties of the materials before you begin to guide their discoveries.

Guiding Children's Actions

1. Work with a small group of children and the three tubs of water, rice, and sand. Have one child close his or her eyes while the others choose a tub for the child to touch. After the child puts a finger in the tub, ask him or her to identify the contents. Ask how the child knew it was water, rice, or sand.

2. After everyone has had a turn identifying the contents of a tub by touch, talk about how the three materials are alike and different.

3. Introduce the experience chart. Work together to fill in the chart with descriptive words about the three materials. Write the words children use to describe the materials beneath the labels. You can focus their observations using questions such as these:

   - How do water, rice, and sand feel different?

   - What happens when you blow on water, rice, and sand? Do they move differently?

   - What happens when you drop something into each of the tubs?

   - What happens when you stick a dry finger into rice, sand, and water? Does water, rice, or sand stick to your finger? (Provide paper towels so that the children can stick a dry finger into each cup.)

   - In which tubs can you see the bottom? Can you see through water, sand, or rice?

   - How is the color of water, sand, and rice different?

Stretching Their Thinking

Ask the children if they think a cup of water weighs more or less than a cup of sand. Use a balance scale to find out.

Let the children explore on their own how the weight of water compares to other materials of their choosing. Can they find something that weighs as much as the water?

Waterflow

Investigation
Observing how water flows.

Skills
Predicting ◊ Observing reactions ◊ Drawing conclusions ◊ Testing hypotheses

Materials
Wash tubs; water play equipment: plastic funnels, clear plastic tubing, bottles, margarine tubs, containers of various sizes and shapes; corks; watering can; sponges; food coloring.

Setting Up
Set up a science center for water play. Set out the wash tubs, the watering can filled with water colored with food coloring, and the water play equipment. Cover the table with a plastic cloth and provide sponges for clean up, as the children will undoubtedly experience spills during this activity.

Starting Out

Let the children explore the materials on their own for a while before you begin directing their discoveries.

Guiding Children's Actions

1. Give each child a piece of tubing stopped with a cork in one end. Pour a little colored water through a funnel into the other end of the tubing, then put a cork on that end. Ask the children where the water will go.

2. Let the children explore the water flow while holding both ends of the tubing. Tell them to raise or lower one or the other end of the tubing and then see where the water goes. They should notice that the water always goes to the lowest part of the tubing.

3. Next, connect a piece of plastic tubing to a funnel on one end and to a large empty soda bottle on the other end. The top of the bottle should be above the funnel; the tubing should curve up and into the bottle.

4. Tell the children that you are going to pour a cupful of water into the funnel. Ask them where they think the water will go. Will it go into the bottle?

5. When everyone has had a chance to predict the results, pour a cupful of water into the funnel and observe with the children that the water does not reach the bottle. Ask them if there is anything they can do to get the water to go up into the bottle.

6. Have the children make a similar structure and experiment to find out. Some children may try to blow the water into the bottle. Others may try to pour more and more water into the funnel. A few may siphon the water into the bottle by sucking on the bottle end of the tubing and then putting the tube back into the bottle. Still others may discover that they can lift the funnel and the water will go into the bottle.

7. As the children make their discoveries, have them share their findings with the others in the group.

Stretching Their Thinking

Make other kinds of constructions with the water play equipment and see if the children can predict where the water will go. One possibility is to build a tower with containers, some with holes poked in them and others without holes. See if the children can predict where the water will go if it is poured into the top container.

Water Visions

Investigation
Exploring how things look through and on water.

Skills
Comparing shape and size ◊ Describing differences ◊ Observing changes

Materials
Clear plastic cups; pitcher of water; straws.

Setting Up
Prepare a table with the materials listed above.

Starting Out

Give each child two clear plastic cups, one empty and one three-quarters full of water. Have the children look through the two cups at objects in the room and compare the images. Ask:

- Can you see through both cups? (Yes.)

- Do things on the wall look different through the water? How are they different? (They are backward. They look curved and fuzzy.)

- Do things on the ground look different through the water? (They are not backward or curved.)

- How does the size of the images compare? (They are smaller through the water.)

Encourage the children to explore other things in the room that look different through a cup of water. Have them share their findings with the other children.

Guiding Children's Actions

1. Give each child a pair of straws to put in a cup. Ask the children if they can see any differences between how the pairs of objects look in the water versus how they look in the empty cup. Use questions like the following:

   - How do the straws look different? (The straw in the water looks as if it bends when it goes into the water.)

   - Does it really bend? How can you tell?

   - How does the size of the straws compare?

2. Let the children find pairs of plastic objects to place in the two cups. Encourage them to compare the images and share their findings with the other children.

3. Have the children see if they can find a mirror image of their faces by looking down into the water in the cup. Have them describe their reflections. Guide them with questions like:

   - Tell us about the face you see in the water. Is it rightside up or upside down?

   - Do you see more than one face?

   - What else can you see?

Stretching Their Thinking

Visit a pond or lake, or find a puddle on the playground after a rain. Look in the water with the children and ask them to describe what they see. Can they see their own reflections? What else can they see? Can they see things sticking out of the water? Do they look bent? Suggest that they throw a pebble into the water and watch to see how the reflection changes.

Mixers

Investigation

Finding out how different cooking ingredients mix with water.

Skills

Observing changes ◇ Using all the senses ◇ Comparing ◇ Describing different reactions ◇ Graphing

Materials

Cooking ingredients such as flour, cocoa, sugar, salt, pepper, baking soda, powdered milk; labels; spoons; clear plastic cups; stirring sticks; pitcher of water; bucket; Sorting Mat.

Setting Up

Set up a table with containers of dry ingredients. Next to each container place a small amount of the material in a plastic cup and provide a spoon for each. Also have available cups half-filled with water and stirring sticks. Have the Sorting Mat available for use later.

Starting Out

Introduce the table to the children. Give each student a stirring stick and a clear plastic cup filled about halfway with water. Identify each dry ingredient and have each child choose one to work with. Explain that the spoons are to be used for measuring only, not for stirring or tasting.

Guiding Children's Actions

1. Ask the children to guess what they think would happen if they mixed their ingredient with water.

2. Have them place a spoonful of their ingredient into their cup of water and stir for several minutes. As they do so, encourage them to look closely at the changes in the water. Ask:

   • What happened to the water?

   • What color is the water now? Is it the same color as the ingredient you added?

   • Which ingredients dissolved (disappeared) when you stirred them in the water?

   • Which cup is the clearest? Which is the darkest?

   • Which things mixed easily with water? Which things did not mix easily?

   • When salt is stirred into water, does it disappear? Does the water taste of salt even though you cannot see the salt in the water?

   • Did any of the ingredients create bubbles?

3. Let the ingredients sit for a while, then ask:

   • Which cups of water look alike now? How could you group together the ones that are alike?

   • Which ingredients are settling to the bottom of the cup?

4. Introduce the Sorting Mat. Work with the children to put together the solutions that are alike in some way. Have the children place the cups on the Sorting Mat and then work together to give names to the groups of solutions.

Stretching Their Thinking

Let the children explore on their own how each of the ingredients mixes with water. Have the children strain the various solutions through sieves lined with cheesecloth. Ask them to find out which solutions leave a residue on the cheesecloth or the bottom of the cup. Have them examine and describe the residue.

Salt And Sand

Investigation
Comparing how sand and salt mix with water.

Skills
Comparing color, shape, and size ◊ Using the sense of taste, touch, and sight ◊ Using hand lenses ◊ Observing reactions ◊ Inferring

Materials
Hand lenses; salt; sand; water pitcher; clear plastic cups; stirring sticks; funnels; coffee filters or cheesecloth.

Setting Up
Set up a table with a quantity of salt and sand. Also have hand lenses available, clear plastic cups, a pitcher of water, and stirring sticks. Line funnels or sieves with cheesecloth or a coffee filter.

Starting Out

Have the children compare the salt and sand using their hand lenses. Discuss the color, size, and shape of the granules, concluding that while the color differs, the size and shape of the granules is similar. Then have the children work in pairs. Have one child close his or her eyes while the other chooses salt or sand for that child to touch. Challenge the children to identify the substance using only their sense of touch.

Guiding Children's Actions

1. Give each child a cup of tap water. Have them stir in some salt and then some sand and observe how the substances mix with water.

2. Have them strain the mixture into a clean plastic cup through a funnel or sieve lined with cheesecloth or a coffee filter.

3. Have them examine and describe the residue in the cheesecloth or filter.

4. Have them examine the water mixture. Talk about their observations with questions like these:

   • What happens to salt when it is stirred in the water? (It disappears in the water.)

   • What happens to sand when it is stirred in the water? (It swims around in the water.)

   • What happens to the sand when you stop stirring? (It settles to the bottom of the cup.)

   • What do you see on the cheesecloth when the liquid is poured through the strainer? (The sand.)

   • How does the liquid look different after the sand is strained? (It looks clear.)

   • What do you think happened to the salt when the liquid was poured through the strainer? What makes you think that way?

Stretching Their Thinking

Collect some water at a pond, lake, or ocean beach and have the children strain it. What do they see?

Have the children experiment with mixing water with other substances and then strain the mixtures and solutions to see if any residue appears on the cheesecloth or filter. Have them sort the substances into those that produce a residue and those that do not.

Sweet Or Sour

Investigation
Combining ingredients to make lemonade.

Skills
Observing changes ◇ Using all the senses ◇ Measuring ◇ Displaying data

Materials
Lemons; clear plastic cups; citrus reamers; sugar (or honey); teaspoons; stirring sticks; Data Sheet #1, (see Management Guide).

Setting Up
Prepare a table for making lemonade. Have citrus reamers available and one lemon per child. Put out a bowl and spoon for the juice. Put out a bowl of sugar with a teaspoon. Put out enough half-cups of water for each child to have one, and stirring sticks. Prepare multiple copies of Data Sheet #1 and set aside.

Starting Out

Explain to the children that they will be making lemonade today. Begin by having them squeeze some lemons (at least one per child) so that you will have enough juice for the exploration. When the lemons are squeezed, set out a bowl of sugar near the juice.

Guiding Children's Actions

1. Give each child a stirring stick and a cup of water. Tell them to count out three spoonfuls of the lemon juice and pour it into their cups of water. Have them stir and then taste the mixture. Ask:

    • How does the cup of water look different now?

    • How does it taste?

    • How does it smell?

2. Next, have the children put spoonfuls of sugar in their cups, one spoonful at a time. Have them stir until the sugar is dissolved, and taste a drop or two after each spoonful has been added. Discuss how the drink looks, tastes, and smells.

3. Challenge the children to add spoonfuls of sugar or lemon juice (one spoonful at a time) until the lemonade tastes the way they like it. As they work, ask questions such as these:
    • How does the drink taste now?

    • How could you make it taste sweeter? sour?

    • After you stir the lemonade, can you see the sugar in it? Can you see the lemon juice in it?

    • Can you still taste the sugar after it dissolves (disappears)?

4. End the activity by having the children drink their creations.

5. Have the children make another cup of lemonade. This time, have them fill in Data Sheet #1 to show the number of spoonfuls of sugar and lemon juice they use to make their lemonade. As they work on making their lemonade, have them color in one spoon for every spoonful of sugar or lemon juice they add.

Stretching Their Thinking

Add a spoonful of baking soda to the lemonade. Have the children describe what happens—what they see and hear. The baking soda causes the lemon mixture to fizz and bubble up, causing a foamy head to appear at the top of the cup. Soon the fizzing sound dies down but the bubbles remain.

Hot Or Cold Chocolate

Investigation
Comparing how ingredients dissolve in hot versus cold water.

Skills
Measuring ◇ Observing changes ◇ Comparing results ◇ Using a thermometer

Materials
Cocoa; sugar; salt; powdered milk; four bowls; hot drink paper cups; measuring spoons; stirring sticks; pitcher of ice water; kettle of boiling water; hot plate; thermometers; Data Sheet #2, (see Management Guide).

Setting Up
On a table set out four bowls in which you have placed the ingredients for making a chocolate drink—salt, sugar, cocoa, and powdered milk. Place a teaspoon in all but the salt bowl. Also set out the pitcher of ice water, the kettle of boiling water, the stirring sticks, and cups. Keep the kettle warm on a hot plate.

Starting Out

Introduce the drink-mixing table and tell the children that they will be making a chocolate drink today. Look over the ingredients on the table and be sure children can identify each.

Guiding Children's Actions

1. Work with groups of about four children at a time. Give each child two cups. Have them mix the ingredients for the chocolate drink in each of the cups. Tell them to put 1 teaspoon of cocoa, 2 teaspoons of sugar, 1 teaspoon of milk, and a pinch of salt in each cup.

2. Then ask them what they think will happen if they pour hot water into one cup. What will happen if they pour cold water into the other cup? Discuss their predictions.

3. Then pour hot water into one cup and cold water into the other cup and have the children stir. Have them compare how the ingredients mix with the water. Ask:
   - How is the cold water mixture different from the hot water mixture? (The cold mixture has lumps and bubbles in it. The hot mixture is easier to stir.)
   - In which cup do the ingredients mix best?
   - Which cup would you prefer to drink?

4. Conclude that the mixture dissolves best in hot water. End the activity by having the children drink the hot chocolate they have made.

Stretching Their Thinking

Show the children Data Sheet #2. Have the children use thermometers to measure the temperatures of the two cups of chocolate. Have them draw a red line on the thermometers shown on the Data Sheets to indicate how warm or cold the drinks were. They could also draw a picture of the chocolate mixtures in each of the cups.

Oil Bubbles

Investigation
Observing how oil mixes with water.

Skills
Comparing ◇ Observing changes ◇ Describing interactions ◇ Comparing time

Materials
Food coloring; cooking oil; clear plastic cups; jug of water; stirring sticks; clear plastic bottle or jar with tight lid or cork.

Setting Up
Set up a table with plastic cups and stirring sticks. Have food coloring available, a pitcher of water, a cup of cooking oil. Have a clear jar with a tight-fitting lid available. A bottle for mixing salad oil is a possibility.

Starting Out

Have the children work in pairs. Give each pair a plastic cup and a stirring stick. Have the first pair mix a small amount of oil and food coloring, the second mix a small amount of water and food coloring, and the third a small amount of oil and water. Get the children to compare the way the materials mix by asking:

- Does the food coloring mix easily with the water? (Yes.) With the oil? (No.)
- Does oil mix easily with water? (No.)

Conclude that different materials mix in different ways.

Guiding Children's Actions

1. Work together to make a bubble bottle. Mix food coloring, water, and oil in the bottle or jar with the tight-fitting lid. For a one-quart jar, you might use 3 cups of water, a few drops of food coloring, and one-half cup of oil. Have the children close the lid tightly and explore how the three materials mix.

2. Ask them if there is any way they can get the oil to mix with the water. They could try shaking the bottle or turning it upside down. Discuss what the oil looks like, what it does, and how it moves. Guide children with these questions:
   - Does the oil ever completely disappear (dissolve) in water? (No.)
   - What happens when you shake the bottle? (Bubbles form.)
   - What happens to the bubbles? (They travel to the top of the bottle.)
   - What happens when you turn the bottle upside down? (The bubbles still travel up.)
   - What happens when you let the bottle sit for a while? (The oil forms a layer on the top.)
   - What happens when you turn the bottle upside down slowly? (Bubbles break off and climb to the top.)

3. Let the children explore the bubble bottles on their own.

4. When one of the children discovers something interesting, have them describe what they did and what they observed so that the others can do it too.

Stretching Their Thinking

Have the children compare how long it takes for the oil layer in their bubble bottles to get to the top after the bottle has been turned upside down. Ask, "How can you get your layer of oil to the top fastest?" Have the children turn over their bottles when you say "go." They can turn the bottles upside down in any way they wish. Some may want to turn it upside down slowly while others might decide to shake the bottle as they turn it upside down. Have the children signal when all the oil is at the top of the bottle. Discuss which bottle "won" and how it was turned upside down.

Soak Ups

Investigation
Finding things that absorb and things that repel water.

Skills
Observing reactions ◊ Testing hypotheses ◊ Classifying

Materials
Eye droppers; cups of water (colored water, if preferred); materials (paper, waxed paper, rubber, aluminum foil, plastic, cardboard, rubber, terry cloth towel, ceramic tile, Styrofoam, cotton, paper towel, metal, typing paper, coffee filters, newsprint, tissue paper, cloth, and so on); Sorting Mat; sponge; rain hat.

Setting Up
Place cups of water (colored lightly with food coloring, if desired), and eye droppers on the table. Spread out the materials listed above on the table as well. Have the two-column side of the Sorting Mat ready.

Starting Out

Display the sponge and the rain hat and ask the children to predict what would happen if you poured some water on the sponge. What would happen if you poured some water on the rain hat? After the children make their predictions, have them watch as you actually pour a little water on each object. Have the children describe what they observe. (Water soaked into the sponge, but it fell off the hat.) Display the Sorting Mat, and place the sponge in one column and the rain hat in the other column of the mat.

Guiding Children's Actions

1. Direct the children's attention to the collection of materials and ask which things they think would soak up water like the sponge.

2. When a child makes a suggestion, test it by having the child place a few drops of water on the material with an eye dropper. Have the children observe how the materials soak up the water. Explain that materials that soak up water should be placed below the sponge on the Sorting Mat. Materials that do not soak up water should be placed below the rain hat. Have a child place the material in the proper column of the Sorting Mat.

3. Then ask: Who can find something that they think will not soak up water? Have someone test a suggestion as described above and place the object on the Sorting Mat. Continue in a similar manner with the other objects in the collection. Ask questions such as these to focus the children's observations:

   • Did it soak all the way through? How can you tell?

   • What shape is the wetness?

   • Did this material take longer to soak up the water?

   • What does the water look like when it does not soak into the material? (It forms beads or buttons of water.)

   • What shape are the beads of water? (Round.)

Stretching Their Thinking

Let the children make crayon resist drawings. Have them draw a design with crayons on a piece of absorbent paper. For best results, encourage them to press down on the crayons and fill in large areas rather than make outlines with the crayons. When the drawing is finished, have them brush a thin watercolor wash over the entire paper. Discuss the results with these questions:

   • What happens to the watercolor wash when it is brushed over the crayon? (Beads of watercolor appear.)

   • Does the crayon soak up the watery paint? (No.)

   • Does the paper soak up the watery paint? (Yes.)

Water Beads

Investigation
Observing the movement of water droplets.

Skills
Describing attributes ◇ Observing reactions ◇ Comparing

Materials
Hand lenses; waxed paper; straws; toothpicks; food coloring; eye droppers.

Setting Up
Prepare pieces of waxed paper (6″ × 6″) and a cup of water colored lightly with food coloring. Place the straws, toothpicks, and hand lenses on the table.

Starting Out

If nature cooperates, begin the activity by having the children observe raindrops falling on the classroom window. Have them follow a drop as it falls down the windowpane and observe what happens when it collides with another droplet. Provide hand lenses, and ask the children to describe what they see. They may comment on the size and shape of the droplets or the reflections they see in the drops. Ask questions to encourage their observations:

- Are all the drops the same size?
- What is the sound of the drops on the window?
- How do the drops move?
- Do all the drops move the same way?
- Can you see through a raindrop?

Guiding Children's Actions

1. Give each child a piece of waxed paper and place a few drops of water on it.

2. Tell the children they may use any of the materials on the table. Guide their discoveries with questions such as these:
   - Can you make the drop wiggle?
   - What shape is the drop when it is not moving? (Round, like half a ball.)
   - How can you move the drop? (Blow on it with a straw.)
   - Does the shape of the drop change when it moves? (Yes. It becomes tear-shaped.)
   - Who can find a way to make one big drop?
   - What happens when two drops bump together? (They become one bigger drop.)
   - Who can find a way to make lots of little drops?

3. Let the children explore the drops on their own. As the children discover something interesting about the drops, have them describe what they did and what they observed, so that the others can do it too.

Stretching Their Thinking

Let children use what they have learned about the movement of water droplets on waxed paper to create some interesting artwork on another type of paper.

Give each child a piece of semiabsorbent paper (typing paper works well). Have some cups of colored water available and an eye dropper. Let the children put a drop of color on their papers and then blow the drop so that it travels to the other side of the paper. They can turn the paper to make the branches go in different directions. When they have blown a drop dry, they can try one or more drops of different colors. Discuss the process:

- Do the drops travel in a straight line?
- Do the drops travel like raindrops on the window?
- What happens when two drops bump into each other?

Talk about how the drops travel differently on the typing paper as compared to the waxed paper.

Color Dips

Investigation
Exploring the soaking capacity of materials.

Skills
Describing designs ◇ Testing hypotheses ◇ Evaluating outcomes

Materials
Saucers of food coloring; paper towels; clothesline and clothespins.

Setting Up
Cover a table with newspaper or a plastic cloth and on it place several dishes of food coloring in various colors (red, blue, and yellow are best) diluted with a small amount of water. Make a supply of paper towels available.

Starting Out

Show the children how to make Color Dips: Fold a paper towel several times, then dip a corner or side of the paper towel in a color. Watch as the color soaks into the towel.

Repeat with other sides or corners until the paper towel is soaked with different colors. Then unfold the towel to see what the design looks like. For the best display of the colors, hang the Color Dip on a clothesline in front of a window where light will shine through it.

Guiding Children's Actions

1. When each of the children has made at least one Color Dip, talk about the colors that were created and the symmetry of the design. Ask:

   - What colors have you made?

   - Can you find parts of the design that are the same?

   - If I cut your design in two, would the two parts look the same?

   - How did you make your design?

2. Ask the children what other kinds of materials they think they could use to make designs like the ones created with the paper towels.

Stretching Their Thinking

Provide materials such as waxed paper, typing paper, paper towels, coffee filters, newsprint, tissue paper, cotton cloth, sheets of cellophane, each folded several times. Have the children experiment with the various materials to decide which materials will make Color Dips and which do not. Discuss the results with questions like these:

   - Do you think the coffee filter will soak up the food coloring?

   - Why is a paper towel better than the waxed paper for making pretty designs with the food coloring? (The waxed paper does not soak up the color.)

   - Does tissue paper soak up the color? (Yes.)

   - Is it a good material for the art project? Why not? (It soaks up too much of the water.)

Changes

Investigation
Finding out how things change when they are soaked in water.

Skills
Observing changes ◊ Comparing size and texture ◊ Predicting outcomes ◊ Classifying ◊ Creating experience charts

Materials
Pairs of objects: rubber bands, crackers, raisins, toothpicks, hard candies, nails, noodles, plastic paper clips, cardboard; jar lids (or shallow dishes); measuring cup; pitcher of water; hand lenses; Sorting Mat and Sorting Mat labels, *Change* and *No Change*, (see Management Guide for labels); large piece of paper.

Setting Up
On a table, spread out all the objects listed above. Have one jar lid for each pair of objects. On Day 2 of this activity, you will need the Sorting Mat and labels and a large piece of paper ruled off in columns.

cracker	raisin	noodle	life saver	bean	cardboard
soggy mushy soft falls apart bigger	fatter lighter color	softer bends easier wider whiter	colors the water	fatter wrinkled skin is breaking off	weaker softer breaks apart darker

Starting Out

Show each of the objects and ask the children what they think will happen to it when it is wet. Encourage a variety of predictions and then suggest that they soak the objects to find out. Place one of each object in a jar lid or shallow dish with its pair nearby for comparison. Have the children pour some water into each dish. Leave the objects in a location where the children can observe them throughout the day. Make the hand lenses available for looking closely at the wet objects.

Guiding Children's Actions

1. On the following day, gather the children at the science center to see what has happened to the objects. Focus their attention on the differences, if any, between the dry object and its soaked counterpart. Ask:

    • Which things changed?

    • Which things stayed the same?

    • How did the cracker change?

    • Did the hard candy change in the same way?

    • Did the way things changed surprise you?

2. Present the Sorting Mat and labels. Read the column labels, *Change* and *No Change*. Have the children place the objects in the appropriate columns.

3. Next, work with the children to develop an experience chart listing words that describe what happened to the objects that changed. Glue an object such as the dry raisin on to the chart and then ask the children to describe how the object changed. Write the children's words below the object.

4. Continue until all of the objects that changed in any way are included on the chart.

Stretching Their Thinking

Make a pot of split pea or bean soup. Have a child measure out some split peas or beans and pour them into a large cooking pot. Then have another child measure out about twice as much water and pour it into the pot. Encourage the children to watch what happens to the peas or beans over the next four-hour period. Talk about how they have changed after being soaked in water.

The following day, you can cook the peas or beans to make a soup. Have the children cut up vegetables (onions, carrots, celery, and so on) and measure out spices (salt, pepper, bay leaves) to add to the soup. Cook the soup and serve it to the children.

Wet Weights

Investigation
Comparing the weight of wet and dry things.

Skills
Measuring weight ◇ Classifying ◇ Recording data ◇ Drawing conclusions

Materials
Balance scale; pairs of identical objects such as sponges and dish towels; pails or dish pans filled with water; Sorting Mat and Sorting Mat labels, *Wet* and *Dry*, (see Management Guide for labels); Unifix® Cubes.

Setting Up
Set up a science center where you provide pairs of objects that absorb water (paper towels, sponges, terry cloth dish rags, cotton balls) for the students, a bucket of water, and the Sorting Mat labeled *Wet* and *Dry*. Place the balance scale on the table.

Starting Out

Have the children soak one of each pair of objects in water and then place the pairs of objects on the Sorting Mat in the proper columns. As they work, ask them how the wet objects differ from the dry objects. (They are dripping water; they have soaked up water; they are soaking wet; and so on.)

Guiding Children's Actions

1. Have the children predict which object weighs more, the wet object or the dry one. Have them check by weighing the pairs of objects on a balance scale to see if the wet object weighs more than the dry object.

2. Encourage the children to feel the difference, too. They should notice, for example, that a wet towel feels much heavier than a dry towel.

3. After they weigh each pair of objects, they can place a marker like a Unifix® Cube on the Sorting Mat to show whether the wet or the dry object weighed more.

4. After the children have experimented with all of the objects you have made available, encourage them to suggest pairs of objects of their own choosing to weigh when wet and dry.

5. If feasible, test their ideas and add the data to the Sorting Mat. If children choose objects that repel rather than absorb water, they may notice that the scale remains balanced. Discuss why this is so.

6. At the end of the session, discuss the data on the Sorting Mat. Notice that all the markers appear in the *Wet* column. Conclude with the children that objects that have soaked up water weigh more than the same objects when dry.

Stretching Their Thinking

The children might count out two sets of 20 dry beans. Have them soak one of the sets of beans in water overnight. The next day, have them pour off the water and compare the two sets of beans. They should notice that the soaked beans are wrinkled, the skins are breaking off, and they appear to take up much more space. If the children weigh the two bowls of beans on a balance scale, they will also discover that the soaked beans weigh more.

Window 14

Water Painting

Investigation
Observing water evaporate.

Skills
Observing changes ◇ Experimenting ◇ Inferring

Materials
Pails or buckets; large paintbrushes; chalk.

Setting Up
Fill the pails with water and take enough paintbrushes for each child to have one. Set the pails and brushes in an open spot on the playground.

Starting Out

On a warm, sunny day give the children an opportunity to do some water painting on the playground. Before directing their activity, give the children a chance to work freely painting with water and make their own observations. Talk in general about how a fence or wall looks different when it is painted. (It looks wet. It shines.)

Guiding Children's Actions

1. Have the children each make a large wet spot with their brushes and then outline it with a piece of chalk. Then tell them to sit back and watch what happens. Talk about what they observe by asking:

    • What happens to the spot? (It gets smaller and smaller.)

    • Where do you think the wetness goes? (Accept various answers.)

    • Which part of your spot dries first?

    • Whose spot will dry first? Why do you think so?

    • Whose spot will dry last? Why?

    • How could you make your wet spot last longer?

2. Explain to the children that when water disappears into the air, we say that it *evaporates*.

Stretching Their Thinking

Challenge the children to make a spot that will last a long time. They may try painting with water on different materials. Does water last longer on a wooden fence or on pavement? Suggest they try painting in the shade. Does a spot dry up faster in the sun or the shade? Have them try using more water on their brushes to see what effect that has. Have the children explain their reasoning and then observe the results.

Wash Day

Investigation
Exploring how long it takes for different materials to become dry.

Skills
Using the sense of touch ◇ Comparing textures ◇ Predicting outcomes ◇ Recording the order of events ◇ Inferring ◇ Using a balance scale

Materials
Small swatches of different fabrics (cotton, silk, wool, rayon, felt, nylon, terry cloth, denim, corduroy, flannel, burlap); plastic washtubs; mild soap; clothesline; clothespins; paste; large sheet of paper for chart.

Setting Up
Prepare 3″ × 3″ swatches of the fabrics listed above. Place them on a table in mixed order. You will also need two plastic tubs, one with soap and water for washing and one with plain water for rinsing. Prepare a chart like the one shown and set it aside.

Starting Out

Display the fabric swatches, and have the children feel them and compare their textures. Discuss which ones are smooth, which are soft, which are rough or bumpy. Have the children take turns identifying a swatch by touch only. Have a child close his or her eyes and pick a swatch from the table, feel it, then put it back on the table. Have the other children scramble the fabrics and challenge the child to open his or her eyes and try to identify the swatch that was touched.

Guiding Children's Actions

1. After the children are familiar with fabrics, have them wash and rinse them. As they work, ask them to compare the way the fabric feels when dry to the way it feels when wet.

2. Have them wring out the swatches and hang them on a clothesline to dry. Make sure the clothesline is placed in a spot where each swatch gets an equal amount of sunlight if near a window or sunlight and wind, if outdoors.

3. Ask the children to predict which fabrics will dry quickest. Which will take the longest time to dry? Have them give reasons for their guesses. Record the predictions.

4. Check the clothesline periodically until all the fabric swatches are dry. As the fabric swatches dry, have children take them off the line and paste them to the chart in the order in which they dried.

5. Compare the results with the children's predictions. Were there any surprises?

6. Discuss why some fabrics, such as terry cloth, take longer to dry. (They absorb more water.)

Stretching Their Thinking

Have the children weigh the swatches after they have been washed, rinsed, and wrung out, to see which swatch weighs the most and which weighs the least. Relate the weight to how quickly the fabric dried. Do the fabrics which are heavier when wet dry more slowly?

Fast Dryers

Investigation
Exploring how wet things become dry.

Skills
Predicting ◇ Using the sense of touch ◇ Comparing conditions ◇ Recognizing cause and effect relationships ◇ Measuring height

Materials
Small cotton cloths or handkerchiefs.

Setting Up
Prepare a table with three cotton handkerchiefs and a tub of water.

Starting Out

Show the children three cotton cloths all the same size. Put all three in water and wring them out. Tell the children you are going to put them outside to dry. Clump one up in a ball, hang another in the sun, hang the third in the shade. Ask the children to predict which one will dry first.

Guiding Children's Actions

1. When one of the cloths has dried, direct the children's attention to the cloths again. Have them compare the dampness of the three cloths. Ask the children why they think the damp cloths are still wet.

2. Give two groups of children wet cloths. Challenge the groups to find a place where their cloths will dry quickly. When the children have chosen their spots, discuss their choices:

   • Why did you hang your cloth rather than lay it flat or crumple it up in a ball?

   • Why did you choose that location to hang your cloth?

   • Can you think of anything you could do to make your cloth dry faster?

3. Some children might suggest blowing on the cloth or pointing a fan at the cloth. Let them experiment in any way that is feasible. Others may have little notion of what will make their cloths dry faster. Encourage them to compare their results with those of other children.

4. The children may notice that parts of the cloths remain damp while other parts are dry. Help them to understand why this might be so. (They might notice that a folded part remained wet, for example.)

Stretching Their Thinking

Give each child two clear plastic cups filled with water. Have them cover one of the cups with foil, then tell them to find a place in the room to put their cups. They can write their names on the cups, if desired. Every day, have them mark the water level. As soon as there is a noticeable difference in the water levels, discuss what they observe by asking:

   • What do you notice about the water level in the cup with a foil top? (It stays the same.)

   • What do you notice about the water level in the other cup? (It keeps going down.)

   • Where do you think the water has gone? (Accept various answers.)

Sink Or Float

Investigation
Finding things that float and things that sink in water.

Skills
Observing reactions ◇ Classifying ◇ Recording data ◇ Comparing weight and size ◇ Conjecturing

Materials
A collection of objects that sink and float such as a cork, washer, Styrofoam, piece of hard wood, piece of balsa wood or a domino, sponge, nail, paper clip, Ping-Pong ball, marble, stone, penny, piece of paper towel, piece of foil; washtub or water table; Sorting Mat and Sorting Mat labels, *Sink* and *Float*, (see Management Guide for labels).

Setting Up
Set out a collection of objects chosen from above and a large plastic tub filled with water. Prepare the two-column side of the Sorting Mat with the labels, *Sink* and *Float*, and place it near the tub.

Starting Out

Show the children the objects on the table. Ask the children which things they think will sink to the bottom of the tub and which will float on the surface of the water. Have them try each of the objects to find out. After they try an object, they should place it in the appropriate column of the Sorting Mat.

Guiding Children's Actions

1. After all the children have had a chance to experiment with the objects in the collection, talk about their findings. Ask:

   • Did anything float for a while and then sink? (If the sponge or paper towel become waterlogged, they will sink.)

   • Why do you think it finally sank? (It was soaked with water.)

   • Did anything sink, then float to the top?

   • Are all the things that floated smaller than the things that sank?

   • Is the marble smaller or larger than the Ping-Pong ball? (Smaller.)

   • In what other ways is the marble different from the Ping-Pong ball? (The Ping-Pong ball is hollow. The marble is heavier.)

   • Are all the things that sank heavier than the things that floated?

   • Why do you think some things float and other things sink?

2. Allow the children to verbalize their guesses on the last question but do not expect them to formulate an accurate conclusion. More experience with the phenomenon is usually necessary before they can infer that the density of the object determines its buoyancy.

Stretching Their Thinking

Challenge the children to find things to add to the collection. Have them find at least one thing that they think will float and one thing they think will sink. Tell them to test their objects by placing them in the water tub. Then have them place the objects in the proper column of the Sorting Mat. Talk about why the children chose the objects and whether their tests yielded any surprises.

Message In A Bottle

Investigation
Trying to sink a bottle.

Skills
Classifying ◇ Measuring ◇ Displaying data ◇ Predicting ◇ Testing hypotheses

Materials
Plastic bottles with tight-fitting lids or corks; washtubs or water table; sand; tablespoons; funnels; Data Sheet #3, (see Management Guide).

Setting Up
Set out a tub of water and have enough plastic bottles for each pair of children. On a separate tray, provide a container of sand, funnels, and tablespoons. Prepare copies of Data Sheet #3 and set aside.

Starting Out

Give each pair of children a plastic bottle. Have the children put their covered bottles into the water. Do they sink or float? (Float.) Ask the children how they think they could sink their bottles. Explore the children's suggestions. Then propose that they try filling the bottles with spoonfuls of sand to see if that causes them to sink.

Guiding Children's Actions

1. Present the tray with the sand materials. Give each child or pair of children a copy of Data Sheet #3. Have them place the bottle in one of the boxes above the spoons and trace around it to show its size.

2. Tell the children to color in a spoon on their Data Sheets for every spoonful of sand they pour into the bottle. Each time they add a spoonful, they should test the bottle to see if it sinks or floats.

3. As they work, talk about the way the bottles sit in the water. As more sand is added, the bottle tends to sit deeper in the water, especially on the weighted side of the bottle. Ask the children what they think will happen when they add another spoonful of sand. Do they think the bottle will sink? How many spoonfuls do they think they will need to add to make the bottle sink?

4. When the bottle sinks, have the children repeat the activity with a different bottle and record the results.

5. When the experiments are completed, post the Data Sheets and discuss the results. Compare the number of spoonfuls of sand it took to sink each of the bottles.

Stretching Their Thinking

Encourage the children to try to sink their bottles with other kinds of materials such as water, pennies, or paper. Which kinds of materials sink the bottles? Which do not? How much of these materials is needed to sink a bottle?

Floating Foil

Investigation
Exploring the shapes of objects that sink and float.

Skills
Describing shape and orientation ◊ Recognizing cause and effect relationships ◊ Testing hypotheses ◊ Classifying

Materials
Plastic spoons; measuring cups; bowls; aluminum foil; Sorting Mat and Sorting Mat labels, *Sink* and *Float*, (see Management Guide for labels).

Setting Up
Put out a tub of water and prepare the two-column side of the Sorting Mat with the labels *Sink* and *Float*. Have plastic spoons, some measuring cups and bowls near the tub. Tear off many pieces of aluminum foil to use later.

Starting Out

Show a plastic spoon and ask the children if they think it will sink or float. Have a child place the spoon in the tub to find out. Then ask: "Can anyone think of a different way to put the spoon in the water?" (They could turn it over and put it in sideways, for example.) Have the children try different ways and check to see whether the spoon sinks or floats. They should discover that whether the spoon sinks or floats depends on what angle and with what force it is placed in the water. They should also notice that the depth at which the spoon sits in the water depends on its orientation.

Have the children explore measuring cups, bowls, and other plastic objects in a similar way.

Guiding Children's Actions

1. Show the children that a small piece of aluminum foil will float on water. Then give each child a piece of foil. Challenge the children to find a way to get the foil to sink. They can try to put it in the water sideways, for example.

2. When a child finds a way to sink the foil, have him or her show the method to the group. Then ask: "Can someone find a different way?"

3. Encourage the children to explore molding the foil into different shapes. As they work, ask questions such as these, when appropriate, to focus their discoveries:

    • How can you put the foil into the water differently so that it will sink?

    • What shapes can you make with the foil?

    • Which shapes seem to make the foil float highest on the water?

    • What if you roll the foil into a long snake? Will it sink or float?

    • If you roll the foil into a tight ball, will it float or sink? What if you roll it into a loose ball?

    • What if you tore your foil into little pieces? Would a tiny piece sink or float?

Stretching Their Thinking

Have the children save interesting shapes they made with the foil. Place them on the Sorting Mat in the appropriate column.

Boats Afloat

Investigation
Constructing boats that float.

Skills
Testing constructions ◇ Comparing size and shape ◇ Solving problems ◇ Predicting ◇ Writing experience stories

Materials
A variety of building materials: scrap wood, Styrofoam, plasticine, aluminum foil, cardboard; glue; plastic tub or water table filled with water; books about boats, or pictures of them; weights (washers or pennies, for example).

Setting Up
Set up a science center where children can explore making boats. Supply a tub of water and the building materials listed above.

Starting Out

Challenge the children to make boats that float. Encourage them to experiment with different materials and to keep checking as they build to make sure that their boats float. Encourage them to use the boat books and pictures for inspiration.

Guiding Children's Actions

1. When the children have finished making their boats, display the weights and ask what will happen if they put some of them into their boats. Will their boats hold the weights? Will the weights sink the boats?

2. Have the children predict how many weights they will be able to put in their boats before they sink. Record their guesses.

3. Have them test their guesses, counting the number of weights they can put in their boats before they sink. If children want to rebuild their boats so that they carry more weight, allow them time to do so.

4. Display all the boats and have the children compare them. Ask:

   • What shapes are the boats?

   • Which is the biggest boat? Smallest? Longest? Flattest? Skinniest?

   • What problems did you run into while making your boats?

   • How did you solve the problems?

   • Which materials do you think are best for making boats? Why?

   • What shapes make the best boats?

5. Float the boats in water for a day or more to see if any sink after extended time in the water. If any sink, talk about why this might have happened. How could the boat construction be improved?

Stretching Their Thinking

Have the children write or dictate experience stories in which they describe their boats and how they were made. Encourage them to describe any problems that arose in construction and how the problems were solved. Let the children illustrate their stories, if desired, and read the boat books to the class.

Ice
Is Nice

Investigation
Comparing ice and water.

Skills
Using all the senses ◊ Describing differences ◊ Creating experience charts ◊ Comparing shape ◊ Observing changes ◊ Comparing temperature

Materials
Small paper cups; pitcher of water; food coloring; dishes; glasses of tap water.

Setting Up
Set out enough paper cups for each child to have two. Arrange the other materials on the table in an inviting manner. Prepare a two-column experience chart, labeled *Water* and *Ice*, for use on Day 2 of this activity.

Starting Out

Give each child two small paper cups. Tell them to write their names on the cups. Pour some water into each cup and allow the children to put a few drops of food coloring in the water to make a color of their choice. Then put one of the cups in a freezer overnight. Explain to the group that they will be taking a close look at their cups the following day.

Guiding Children's Actions

1. Take the cups out of the freezer the next day and return the ice- and water-filled cups to their owners.

2. Have the children pour the contents of each of their cups into a separate dish and compare the way they look, sound, and feel.

3. Introduce the experience and encourage children to describe their two cups. Write the descriptive words the children use in proper columns. Ask questions like the following to elicit their observations:

    *   How did the water pour differently from the ice? (Water splashes and flows. Water is runny.)
    *   What sound did the water make when you poured it into the bowl? (Swish.)
    *   What sound did the ice make when you poured it into the bowl? (Clunk.)
    *   How does the ice feel different from water? (The ice is cold and hard. The water is warmer and softer.)
    *   What happens when you touch the water? (Your finger gets wet.)
    *   What about when you touch the ice?
    *   Is the color different? (The water is the same color all over. With the ice, the color is in the middle.)
    *   In what other ways does the ice look different? (The ice has cracks in it. You can see through the water.)
    *   How is the shape different? (The ice is the shape of the cup. The water doesn't have a shape.)
    *   Which is easier to pick up with your hands—ice or water? (The ice can be picked up, but the water cannot.)
    *   How is the ice changing? (It is melting.)

Stretching Their Thinking

Have the children pour their ice cube and their water into a glass of plain tap water. Talk about what they observe. They should notice several things: the ice floats in the water; the ice makes the tap water colder (You can verify this with a thermometer, if desired.); the colored water from the ice cube flows down to the bottom of the glass. They may also notice that the ice cube melts faster in the water.

Popsicles

Investigation
Making popsicles in various containers and comparing how fast they freeze.

Skills
Measuring ◇ Comparing volume ◇ Observing effects ◇ Inferring causes

Materials
Kool-Aid® or juice concentrate; pitcher; water; paper cups; popsicle sticks; paper squares.

Setting Up
Gather the materials and place them on a table in preparation for making popsicles.

Starting Out

Begin by having the children mix up a pitcher of Kool-Aid or juice, following the instructions on the package. Then give each child two paper cups, two popsicles sticks, and two paper squares. Tell them they can each make two popsicles, but each one should be a different size. Have the children pour an amount of the flavored drink into each container. Next, tell them to write their names on the paper squares and mark the level of the liquid on the outside of each cup. Finally, have them poke each popsicle stick through the center of the paper square and place the stick in the cup.

Guiding Children's Actions

1. Put the cups in the freezer and wait until the smaller amount is frozen but the larger one is not. (You will have to time the activity so that this will happen during the school day.)

2. Gather the children to examine their popsicles. Talk about what they see. Ask:

   - How have the popsicles changed?
   - Which one is frozen? (The smaller one.) Why do you think it is frozen and the other one is not? (Larger popsicles take longer to freeze.)
   - What do you notice about the frozen popsicle?
   - How is the one that is not frozen different?
   - Where does the popsicle appear to freeze first?
   - How can the popsicle that is not frozen be made to freeze? (Give it more time in the freezer.)

3. Draw attention to the line the children drew on their cups. They will notice that the frozen liquid is above the line since water expands when it is frozen.

4. End the activity by letting the children eat their popsicles.

Stretching Their Thinking

Let the children try making popsicles or plain ice in various kinds of molds—small gelatin molds, foil cupcake liners, jar lids, and so on. The children may have some difficulty predicting what will make good ice molds, but they will learn a lot in the process. The following day, have the children take their popsicles out of the freezer and place them on a pie pan or cookie sheet. Let them show their creations and see if the class can guess what was used to make the popsicle.

Fast Or Slow

Investigation

Comparing how long it takes ice cubes to melt.

Skills

Observing changes ◇ Comparing elapsed time ◇ Predicting ◇ Testing hypotheses ◇ Measuring temperature

Materials

Ice cubes; cups.

Setting Up

The day before doing the activity, make a quantity of ice cubes. Set up a table with the ice cubes, and cups.

Starting Out

Distribute two cups to each child. Have the children write their names on the cups. Then put an ice cube in each cup and suggest that the children find a place to put the cups. Encourage them to put the cups in different places. As the children find places for their cups, ask:

- What do you think will happen to the ice cubes?

- Do you think that both ice cubes will melt in the same time? About how long do you think it will take?

- Which cube do you think will melt faster? Why?

Guiding Children's Actions

1. Encourage the children to check their ice cubes frequently during the next hour or more.

2. After the ice cubes have melted, talk in a group about the results. Guide children with questions like these:

- Which of your ice cubes melted faster? Why do you think it melted faster? (It was in the sun. It was on the radiator.)

- Where did the ice cubes melt slowest? (In the shade. Outside in the cold.)

- What do you think you might do to get your ice cubes to melt faster?

3. Give each child another pair of ice cubes and two cups. Have the children experiment with putting their cubes in different locations.

Stretching Their Thinking

Encourage interested children to try different ways to make their ice cubes melt faster. Use questions like these to inspire them:

- Does it matter what kind of cup you put your ice in? Would ice melt faster in a clear plastic cup, a paper cup, or a ceramic cup?

- Would it melt faster if it were crushed?

- If something were added to the water (juice, salt, sugar), would it melt faster or slower?

Ice Keepers

Investigation
Finding ways to keep ice from melting.

Skills
Predicting ◇ Comparing time ◇ Recording data ◇ Sequencing ◇ Drawing conclusions ◇ Using all the senses

Materials
Materials such as dish towels, aluminum foil, Styrofoam packing, tissue paper, various kinds of fabrics, plastic wrap, sandbags, bean bags; ice cubes; dishes or plates.

Setting Up
The day before doing the activity, freeze a supply of ice cubes. Prepare a chart like the one shown below. On the day of the activity, set out the materials on a table.

minutes	material
10	
20	
30	
40	
50	
60	

Starting Out

Have the children choose partners for this activity. Explain that you will be giving each pair of children an ice cube. Tell them that their job is to think of a way to keep it as long as possible. They can use any of the materials you make available. Give the children a few minutes to talk with their partners about what they could do and decide on a plan.

Guiding Children's Actions

1. When the partners are ready, give them an ice cube in a bowl or plate. Try to pass out the ice cubes quickly so that everyone will have about the same amount of time to cover up their ice cubes with the materials. Have the partners keep their ice cubes near them so that they can check them.

2. Introduce the experience chart to the children. Set a timer to go off every 10 minutes, and have the children check their ice cubes. If a cube has completely melted, have the partners put their ice-keeping material on the chart.

3. When all of the materials are on the chart, you will have a record of how long the materials kept the ice cubes from melting. Discuss the results with questions such as these:

   • Which material was the best ice cube keeper?

   • Which was the poorest?

   • Did the material you chose work well? Why or why not?

Stretching Their Thinking

Distribute some orange juice or other flavored drink to the children. Ask them if they think that ice will melt faster or slower in the drink than it does in an empty cup. Have the children put an ice cube in their drink and in an empty glass and watch to find out. (The one in the juice is likely to melt much more quickly than the one in the empty glass.) While the ice melts, the children can listen to the crackling sounds it makes and watch the melting process. When one of the ice cubes is completely melted, have the children report their findings. Then they can drink their juice.

Bubble Prints

Investigation
Making prints of bubbles.

Skills
Measuring ◇ Comparing number and length ◇ Describing size and shape ◇ Experimenting ◇ Recording measurements

Materials
Shallow trays, dishes, or lids; dishwashing liquid; tempera paint; pitcher of warm water; tablespoon; one-half cup measure; straws; absorbent paper.

Setting Up
On a table, set out a tablespoon, some dishwashing liquid, a ¹/₂-cup measure, a pitcher of warm water, and a shallow tray for each small group or pair of children. Also have available a supply of straws and sheets of absorbent paper.

Starting Out

Have the children prepare the bubble solution. Have them measure 1 tablespoon of dishwashing liquid for each half cup of warm water until the tray is about half-filled with the solution. Then tell them to choose a color of tempera paint, add it to the solution, and stir until a rich color is achieved.

Guiding Children's Actions

1. Give the children straws and have them blow small bubbles all over the shallow trays. Advise them to blow out rather than sucking in the straws; otherwise they may get a taste of the soap in their mouths.

2. As the children work, ask them questions like these to focus their observations:

    • What is the best way to make the bubbles?

    • How can you make lots of layers of bubbles?

    • How high can you make your layers of bubbles?

3. Let the children capture their bubbles by placing a piece of absorbent paper lightly on the bubbles.

4. Then, when the prints have dried, have the children trace the sides of some of the bubbles in the print, counting the number of sides as they trace. Discuss the results with questions like these:

    • How many sides do the bubbles have?

    • Do they all have the same number of sides?

    • Are the sides all the same length?

Stretching Their Thinking

You might have the children experiment with the proportions of dishwashing liquid, water, and paint they use to make the bubble solution. Does adding more soap or more paint make better prints? After they experiment, have them write or dictate a recipe for a bubble solution.

Bigger Bubbles

Investigation
Making large bubbles in a pan.

Skills
Describing shape and color ◊ Describing tactile sensations ◊ Comparing size ◊ Measuring length ◊ Creating experience charts

Materials
Dishwashing liquid; glycerine (optional); trays; straws; rulers (optional).

Setting Up
Set out trays of bubble solution for groups of children to use. Pour in about 2 tablespoons of dishwashing liquid for each cup of water. Add a few drops of glycerine, if desired, to make the bubbles stronger and last longer.

Starting Out

Assign a child to a tray and give him or her a straw. Challenge the children to make one very large bubble in their trays.

Guiding Children's Actions

1. If a child is successful in producing a large bubble, have him or her describe how it was made to the group. If the children do not discover the trick on their own, explain that large bubbles can be made by dipping the straw in the tray, then holding it just above the water and blowing slowly through the straw.

2. After the children have made some large bubbles, talk about what they see. Ask:
   - What shapes are the bubbles?
   - Can you see color in the bubbles? Where is the color? How many colors can you see?
   - What do you think is inside a bubble?
   - Can you see yourself in the bubble? What does your reflection look like?
   - What happens to the image when you get closer? farther away?
   - How are other things in the room reflected in the bubble?
   - What happens when you touch the bubble with dry hands?
   - What happens when you touch the bubble with wet hands? How does the bubble feel? How does the bubble change when you touch it?

Stretching Their Thinking

Have the children compare the size of their bubbles. Some groups of children may be able to measure their bubbles with standard units such as a ruler. Others could measure their bubbles with nonstandard units such as paper clips.

Be A Bubble

Investigation
Examining bubble movement.

Skills
Measuring ◇ Describing movement ◇ Observing changes ◇ Mimicking movement

Materials
Cup; tablespoon; dishwashing liquid; glycerine (optional); bubble frames (or wire to make frames).

Setting Up
Since this is a wet and drippy activity, you may want to set it up outdoors. Give each child a cup half-filled with water. Have them measure and stir in a tablespoon of dishwashing liquid. Add a drop or two of glycerine, if desired, to make the bubbles stronger and last longer. Then distribute bubble frames to each child. You can use commercial plastic frames or you can make frames with wire.

Starting Out

Let the children freely explore the materials before you direct their discoveries. Encourage them to try making bubbles by blowing as well as by waving the frames through the air. The children should notice that in order to make a bubble they must first produce a thin soap film on their frames.

Guiding Children's Actions

1. Have a few children take turns blowing bubbles while the others observe them float through the air.

2. Talk about what they see. Ask:

   - How do bubbles move in the air? Do they turn? How can you tell?
   - Which way are the bubbles moving? Do they all move that way? Why do you think they are moving that way?
   - Can someone think of a way to get a bubble to move a different way?
   - How does the color change as the bubble moves?
   - What makes a bubble break?
   - Can you catch a bubble without breaking it? How?
   - When a bubble lands on your hand, what does it feel like?
   - What happens when a bubble breaks on the ground? What do you see?

Stretching Their Thinking

Play some appropriate music (classical Baroque might be ideal, for example) and have the children move like bubbles. When the music is slow, suggest that the weather is calm; the bubbles are floating softly in the air. As the music gets more frenzied, suggest that a wind is picking up and the bubbles are being tossed by the wind. The children might enjoy bursting their bubble selves as a climax.

Better Bubble Building

Investigation
Finding things that make good bubbles.

Skills
Experimenting ◊ Comparing size, length, and shape ◊ Describing differences ◊ Writing stories

Materials
Bubble-making equipment (paper rolls, paper cups, straws, wire, funnels, clear plastic tubing, metal cookie cutters, clothes hanger, bubble pipes, and bubble wands); plastic tub; dishwashing liquid; glycerine (optional).

Setting Up
Make some bubble-making pipes and wands. To make a pipe, punch a hole in the side of a paper cup and poke a straw through the hole. To make a wand, form one end of some wire into a shape such as a triangle, circle, or square and use the other end as a handle. Set out the tub filled with bubble solution (dishwashing liquid, water, and glycerine).

Starting Out

Let the children freely explore the materials before you begin to guide their discoveries.

Guiding Children's Actions

1. After the children have explored the available equipment for a while, suggest that they look for other materials and other ways to make bubbles. They may find, for example, that they can make a bubble with a Unifix® Cube. Or they might find that they can blow a bubble through the holes in a spatula.

2. When they find things that make good bubbles, have them add the equipment to the table. Things that do not work should be rinsed off, dried, and put back where they were found.

3. You may need to monitor the activity carefully to see that children do not use materials that can be damaged in water. Warn the children not to use glass objects.

4. As the children work, ask questions such as these:
   - Which things make the strongest bubbles? the biggest bubbles?
   - How are the bubbles made with this material (straws, for example) different from bubbles made with this material (bubble pipes, for example)?
   - Which things are easiest to use in making bubbles?
   - Do big bubble makers make bigger bubbles?
   - Can you make a very big bubble with a very small bubble maker?
   - Do square bubble makers (the square wand, for example) make square bubbles? What about bubble makers that are triangles? Are all bubbles round?
   - Will a toilet paper roll make a smaller bubble than a paper towel roll?
   - What if you taped several paper towel rolls together? What kind of bubbles will it produce?

Stretching Their Thinking

Have each child write or dictate a story about the adventures of a bubble. Encourage the children to describe their bubbles and to use their imaginations to tell about what happens to the bubble. Let them illustrate their stories with pictures of their bubbles.

WINDOWS ON BEGINNING SCIENCE: Active Learning for Young Children (Grade PreK-2) by Joan Westley. This extraordinary new hands-on science program will help young children develop a thinking approach to the nature and processes of science. The subject matter is everyday things—water, light, bugs, seeds, sand and rocks, and ramps and wheels, and the approach centers around exploring, observing, recording, and communicating. Clear, detailed, step-by-step instructions for every lesson are presented in six resourcebooks. Each resource book contains more than 25 lessons and includes lists of readily-available, everyday materials, and helpful hints to make preparation simple. A must for the library of every early childhood professional.

Water and Ice (*Cat. No. 56920*)

Insects and Other Crawlers (*Cat. No. 56921*)

Light, Color, and Shadows (*Cat. No. 56922*)

Rocks, Sand, and Soil (*Cat. No. 56923*)

Seeds and Weeds (*Cat. No. 56924*)

Constructions (*Cat. No. 56925*)

Management Guide (*Cat. No. 56930*)

Windows on Beginning Science Complete Materials Kit (*Cat. No. 56933*)

For prices and other information about *Windows on Beginning Science*, please see a current Creative Publications Catalog.

Creative Publications
788 Palomar Avenue ◆ Sunnyvale, CA 94086   Cat. No. 56920